For Matteo, Rachele, Gabriel and Elisa,
with all my love, from grandma Luisa.

To my three little great men, Federico,
Nicolò and Gabriele, with much love. Silvia

English layout: Jessica Aucoin
English translation: Dr. Glenn CJ Byer

Published by
Paulist Press
997 Macarthur Boulevard
Mahwah, NJ 07430

www.paulistpress.com

Library of Congress Cataloging-in-Publication Data available on request.

Originally published by
PAOLINE Editoriale Libri
Via Francesco Albani, 21 - 20149 Milano
www.paoline.it
edlibri.mi@paoline.it

Printed and bound in Hong Kong by Printing Express.

Maria Luisa Eguez

Our Father Is...

Illustrated by

Silvia Colombo

Paulist Press
New York / Mahwah, NJ

You still hear it
whenever kids get together –
everyone tries to outdo each other:

“My dad has a BIG car!”
“Yeah?! My dad’s car is BIGGER than your dad’s!”
“Well, my dad has a RED car!”
“So what?! My dad’s car is REDDER than your dad’s!”

But we all have a Father in Heaven.
What can we say about OUR FATHER?

Our Father

made everything.
He created the planets
one by one.

Our Father

is also a clockmaker
who gives rhythm to the days and
the seasons as they come and go.

Fig. 2.
ODE DE PINDARE.
Premier Morceau de Musique Ancienne
Morceau de Musique Ancienne
Dessus

Our Father
is a painter who invented
all the colours of the rainbow.

Our Father
is a musician who writes symphonies
with water and wind.

Our Father
spoke the Word as a poet,
making the earth, the animals
and the air.

Our Father
is the world's greatest chef,
giving the flavours to
everything we eat,

to the fruits and vegetables
that are our food.

Our Father

is a tailor who sewed seams of mountains
and covered them in clothes of silence
and the purest snow,
made red by the sunrise
and orange at sunset.

Our Father
sweetly caresses
the foothills
so that people and animals
will go to sleep.

Our Father

wakes the valleys in the morning,
sending the winds a little at a time
through the trees and the fields.

Our Father

planted stars like seeds in the sky
so that we could see when
nighttime comes.

Our Father
put sand on the shore
so the sea could play,
and scattered rocks
to give joy to the waves.

Our Father
laughs out loud
when he sees
us happy.

Our Father

makes dreams of the clouds
that then become rivers,
waterfalls and oceans.

Our Father

brings everything to life here
in the garden:
every egg that hatches,
every flower that blooms
and every newborn creature.

Our Father
is a guardian,
with all the angels
at his command.

Our Father
has compassion
for every tear that falls.

Our Father
is against
all kinds of pride
and cruelty,
and he always holds
his little ones
in his embrace.

Our Father
is the strongest of all,
but he never smashes anything.

Our Father
is very patient
and guides everything and everyone
with gentle care – even the littlest ones.

Our Father

is the King of kings
and the Lord of lords,

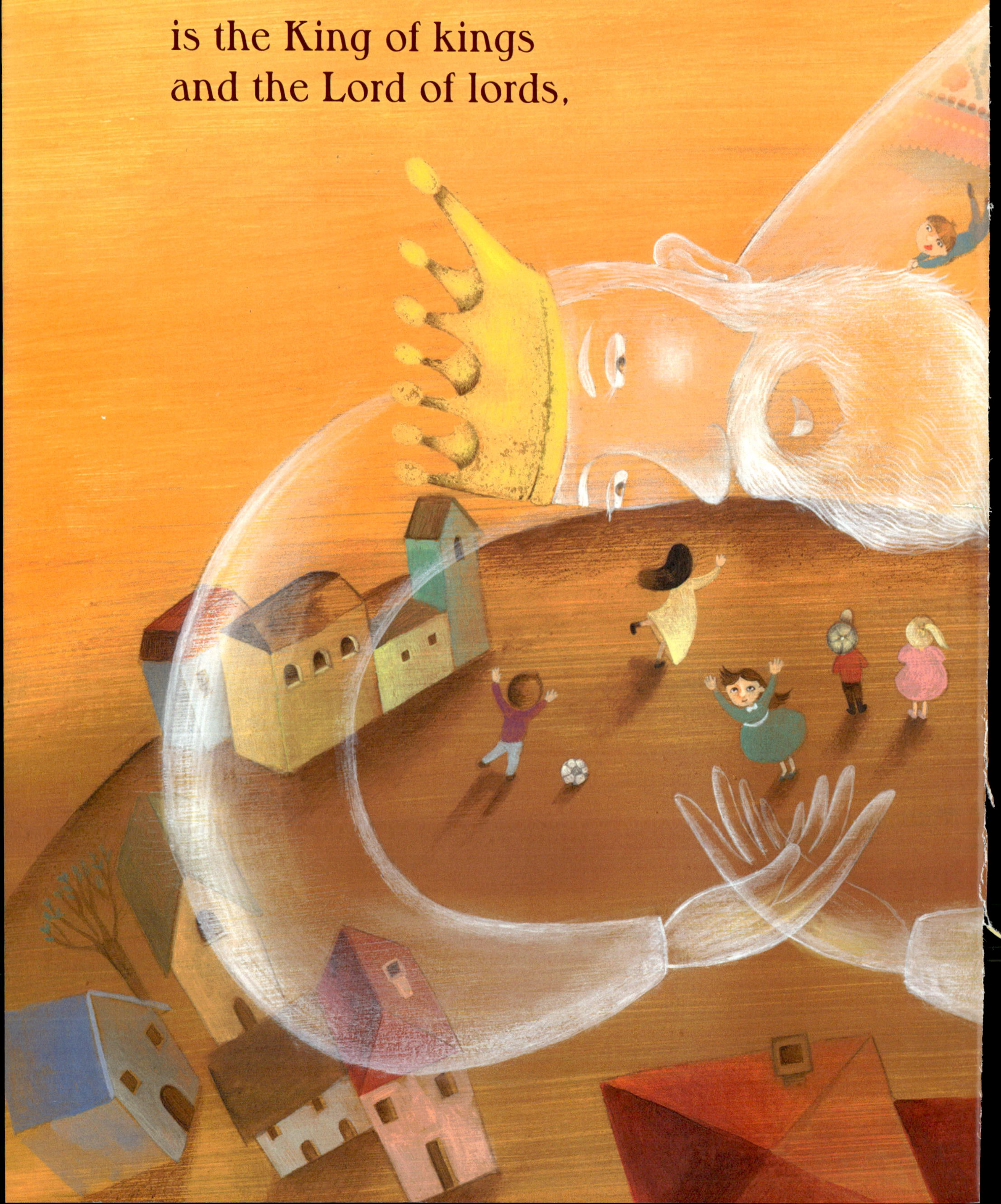

but when
we call on him he says,
"Here I am!"

Our Father
is great.

Our Father
made the universe
all by himself.